Boomercide:
From Woodstock to Suicide

Peter Levitan

Portlandia Press
Portland, Oregon

*For Mary Lee who graciously puts up with
my ideas and Mackenzie and Nick
who should start saving for retirement.*

ISBN: 978-0-9883119-0-9

Portlandia Press
Portland, OR

Editor: Matt Gartland
Cover Design By: Andrew Maudlin

There is but one truly serious philosophical problem,
and that is suicide.

- Albert Camus, *The Myth of Sisyphus*

Table of Contents

Before I Start...

If you are in crisis and are seriously thinking of suicide please contact one of these organizations right now. They are available 24/7.

The National Suicide Prevention Lifeline:
1-800-273-TALK (8255)

The Veterans Crisis Line:
1-800-273-8255

For International suicide hotlines, visit Facebook's Suicide Help Center: http://on.fb.me/sQdcMd

A Personal Perspective On
A Taboo Subject

This book does not promote or advocate suicide. Rather, my objective is to present a review and discussion of suicide from my personal perspective and life-goals, the views of my Baby Boomer cohort and the research I've conducted on the subject.

Know this: I am not an expert on suicide and do not claim to be one. If you are interested in digging deeper into this subject, virtually every fact about suicide as well as expert resources are in your local library and are accessible via Google, Bing or Amazon searches with a click or two.

Internet searches confirm that suicide is a very popular subject. Approximately 7.5 million "suicide" keyword searches were performed on Google's North American website in September 2012. To put this in perspective, there were approximately 13 million searches on the keyword "Obama" in the same month. I find it fascinating that in an election year, suicide is as topical as our sitting President.

I am acutely aware that researching, analyzing and writing about suicide might appear as a form of advocacy. Let me be clear: I am not an advocate. However, I do believe that suicide for sane adults (or more accurately the idea of euthanasia, whether physician-assisted or self-administered) is an increasingly relevant subject worthy of examination. And, to take it one step further, I believe that for me, suicide represents a viable, logical and sane option for the uncertainties inherent in end-of-life planning.

This book explores the genesis and development of my beliefs through reflections of my personal experiences and extensive research. I hope to offer an objective, fact-based overview on the subject of suicide, in particular among older adults, which will provoke a national conversation and bring more attention to end-of-life issues.

I am also aware that for many, suicide is a taboo subject that is better left to the medical community, suicide prevention organizations, the clergy, sociologists, philosophers and even our government. Some people think that shunning or ignoring the subject of suicide is best, believing that any discussion of the subject will lead to an increase in the incidence of suicides.

I respect these opinions but do not agree with them. With more suicides than homicides per year in America, this subject clearly merits more discussion, not less.

I *Am* Going To Kill Myself

Last year I turned 60, sold my advertising agency, watched my two children (21 and 23) begin independent lives and realized that everything that had appeared stable has now changed. It was time to take stock, revaluate and plan for this new and very different life stage. First step, reflection.

Like many Baby Boomers, I have been defined by my career. I've been an executive in New York and London at the largest global advertising agency. I've started two Internet companies, including one of the first online newspapers back in 1995. And I recently sold my Portland, Oregon advertising agency. Since then, I have begun working on a new Internet startup as well as writing eBooks for Baby Boomers. I still do a fair bit of travel. This year alone I've travelled to Thailand where I gave a speech to a newspaper conference, Cambodia where I worked for a month at Aziza's Place, an inner-city residence for wonderful kids and Argentina to visit my daughter at college. I am happily married and live in Portland, Oregon, America's coolest city. Life's been good to me.

Sixty is an interesting age. *Interesting*, in this case, reminds me of the Chinese curse: "may you live in *interesting* times." I am still vital, can link my years of experience to new endeavors and have the freedom to dream and plan for "retirement", whatever the heck that means. However, at 60 I am beginning to feel the effects of age on my body; I look different in the morning mirror, I can't remember the name of the guy I met at last week's party and I wonder at what rate my body is slowing down. With these changes accelerating, I'm left to ponder what the effect of my aging body and mind will have on the future of my physical and financial health. I am beginning to wonder if I can answer this increasingly important question: Can I really make a realistic plan for my future?

Well, it's not foolish to plan, but it may be foolish to believe that all will go according to plan. For example, I can pay a bit more attention when someone tells me his or her name; I can do a few more push-ups and I can load up on sunscreen. But, let's face it, how can anyone plan a perfect post 60-future when there are so many uncertainties: physical and mental health, the state of our economy and, most importantly, having the financial resources to cover my life expectancy. I don't do well with uncertainty.

This is why I have begun to think of suicide as a planning device. The idea of planning a specific end-date helps alleviate this feeling of incertitude and can act as a financial planning tool. This is my deliberate, mindful and reality-based approach to financial planning. I call it rational suicide.

My rational suicide concept is based on the idea that a person could actually make a fully conscious and sensible decision about the benefits of ending one's life on a specific date based on an assessment of his or her future.

I think of it this way…

"Will your future bring you more joy than grief?"

Despite the fact that this form of decision-making is already tacitly embedded in the practice of creating advance health care directives, i.e. living wills, I think that there is a bit of Baby Boomer-driven hedonism in this concept as well: Since I am fully in charge of my life, why can't I choose when and how to die?

The idea of committing suicide is new for me. There have been no suicides in my family, nor have any friends or their relatives committed the act. In fact, the only time that I ever thought about suicide was when I saw a suicide news story or, frankly, whenever I drive over the Golden Gate Bridge. Like most of us, I have attributed the act of suicide to mental illness, serious depression or a very loud call for help. I viewed suicide as an act that could only be committed by a very desperate person. This seems to be both based on fact (yes, depression accounts for most suicides) and how we are programmed by our culture to never imagine that anyone could take his or her own life. Suicide is against our most firmly held moral and religious beliefs. So naturally, there are people that view the compassionate use of physician-assisted suicide as a sinful act that could only be executed by the marginally insane who will then spend eternity in Hell.

But now, as I reevaluate my life's goals and the control (or lack thereof) I have over my future, as well as my personal beliefs, I can't help but feel that there is a broader rationale that is both timely and legitimate.

I am not depressed or insane (I bet they all say that), but I view suicide as a legitimate option. The idea that I might actually consider suicide first occurred to me when I was sitting with my financial advisor. We were crafting my family's financial future shortly after I had sold my business. We reviewed my balance sheet and tried to answer some very important questions. What's our net worth? How long could our money last? Do I still have to work? If so, for how long? Will interest rates and the stock market ever regain momentum? When does it make sense to start to receive Social Security payments? Do I need to establish a very tight budget? What will our health care cost as we age? These are very important financial questions. But, why did they lead a relatively financially secure person to thoughts of suicide? To satisfactorily answer that question, I must set aside my innate sense of privacy and reveal some of my personal relationship with money.

I spent my first eight years living what my parents called a "comfortable" life. We were not fabulously wealthy but we lived in a large apartment on New York's Central Park West across the street from John Lennon's future home. My father had his own business in the Empire State Building; we had a summerhouse and a Cadillac. From my young perspective, this was a very good life. It all came crashing down when I was 8-years-old and my father died from heart failure. In a very short period of time, we had moved to a smaller apartment, my stay-at-home mom went to work full-time and my grandmother moved in to help. Even as my mother tried to mitigate any sense of financial insecurity and take care of a small boy, I quickly realized that things had dramatically changed. I didn't complain that we had less, but it was hard not to notice that my mom was under much more strain. It was a sudden and dramatic change for a boy and I believe that the importance that I now place on being "comfortable" was born at this time.

The good life was resurrected when my mother remarried. But the idea of having financial security to prevent downward spirals became essential, both consciously and unconsciously, to my well-being. To this day, I become anxious when I think about the details of my family's financial position. I realize that I am not the only person that thinks this way; the money = happiness equation resides to a certain extent in all of us. But I have a sense that my personal unease stems from how, as an eight year-old, I watched and internalized my family's turmoil, especially my mother's struggle with the death of a husband and subsequent move to a much lower income status.

These experiences cemented forever my need for financial security, and as such, "comfort" has become an important ingredient in my persona. Thus, having a very rational approach to life, one in which I believe that I am in control, is a key element in driving my happiness. By contrast, not being in control is painful for me. This internal wiring gave rise to my rational suicide idea as I examined our net worth spreadsheets with my financial planner. My predisposition for control made me very conscious of the fact that there are three critical, somewhat variable components that will determine the path of my, and by extension, my family's financial future.

VARIABLE ONE: How much money I have and can expect to earn in the future?

This number is comprised of the payout from the sale of my advertising agency, cash reserves, my home's value, 401K and IRA retirement funds and other investments (very much subject to the vagaries of the markets). Add in future work (an unknown) and eventual Social Security payments to complete the forecast. Despite my strong belief in the need for Social Security reform, I like this entitlement because it helped ease the financial stress after my dad died; I received survivor payments until I was 18. Plus, I am an entitled Baby Boomer after all. I earned it.

VARIABLE Two: How much money will I spend?

Our spending habits are somewhat controllable, as I'd like to think that my wife and I can take a hard look at our finances and plan a budget around them based on choosing where we want to live and what lifestyle we want. Clearly, this is a critical point and the best way that I can approach it in real-time is to assume that we'd like to maintain our current lifestyle which is comfortable but not extravagant.

Now, do we have a budget? No. Should we? Yes. With two global children (one in Budapest, the other in Buenos Aires), just two trips to visit our kids cost us about $6,000 per year. Having a thoughtful budget would help us better prepare for expenses like these.

Spending habits aside, the largest elephant in our financial room is the eventual cost of our senior care arrangements. We are getting first-hand experience with the financial and emotional cost of senior care as we watch our parents and friend's parents live well into their 80s and 90s. The costs can be mind-blowing. According to the insurance company MetLife, the national average annual base rate in an assisted living community is $41,714. This figure increased by 5.6% from 2010 to 2011! The national average daily rate for a private room in a nursing home equals $87,000 per year. Home health aides and homemaker/companion service rates are $20 per hour.

If my wife and I were to move into a shared private room at 85 and lived to 95 we would need approximately $870,000 to cover the cost. Ouch.

VARIABLE THREE: How long will I live?

This is where my financial meeting got very interesting. My advisor matter-of-factly said that life expectancy is the one variable (and it's a huge variable) that we can't control. We are at the mercy of fate. I quickly realized that the randomness of my "sell-by" date is the greatest unknown and the wildest card in my deck. With today's medical advancements, we could live on and on. With this perspective, going broke simply because you lived too long isn't hard to imagine.

The realization that I could outlive any form of intelligent financial planning triggered my control issue anxieties. So, naturally, I began researching the subject of life expectancies in an attempt to reclaim some control. I began simply by exploring whether or not it was possible to gain any reasonable insight at all into my life expectancy. To my great surprise and compulsive delight, I found that there is a growing industry dedicated to determining the key factors that regulate how long we live. I call it the death prediction industry. The death prediction industry studies the obvious factors that influence death including family health histories of cancer, heart attacks, high-blood pressure and other hereditary disorders.

Death prediction institutions are now enhancing their calculations by factoring in our lifestyle habits and personality traits. The leader in this world is the California company Longevity Insight Services (of course they are based in California). Longevity Insight Services' LITE tool, the first bio-psycho-social longevity evaluation tool, is helping industries like insurance and health care gain a more accurate understanding of what drives longevity.

Longevity Insight Services' Howard Friedman is the foremost thought leader in this relatively new science. His groundbreaking book, The Longevity Project, provides compelling linkage data between lifestyle habits and patterns of living and longevity. I am not wholly sure that Mr. Friedman's findings bode well for me as I was a somewhat scattered, attention-deprived kid who became a gregarious ad man (think Mad Men). Such a history and lifestyle apparently leads to an earlier death. As Friedman has written, "The findings clearly revealed that the best childhood personality predictor of longevity was conscientiousness – the qualities of a prudent, persistent, well-organized person – somewhat obsessive and not at all carefree." Apparently, being more nerd-like and less Mad Man-like is the way to go if you want to live longer.

As I continued to reflect on the life expectancy financial planning factor, I started to think through a series of "what-if's" pertaining to my longevity. Will I live to 75, 85, 95, 105? The average for people born in 1951, my birth year, is 68. Really? Only 68? I researched further and discovered that Boomers like me who made it past 60 could expect to live to around 80. Ok, that's better. Add in a generally hearty family history, upper-middle class diet, daily exercise and world-class health care with seemingly unlimited Medicare funds to keep me going strong and I could eventually make it to 100.

The realization that living a long (even too long) life could lead to financial ruin was a very scary wake up call. Given the unknown of when we are going to die, how could anyone, except for the 1%, ever have a legitimately sound financial plan for his or her future? Sure, you could adjust your lifestyle expectations over time to compensate for the longevity variable. But I don't want to scale down to trailer park living. I want to preserve my current lifestyle. That might sound harsh, but it's my truth. At this point, I started to feel really out of control. I grew up thinking I was in charge of my life. Was this just another Baby Boomer myth or could I exert some control over the uncontrollable?

This thought exercise intensified as my financial planning session progressed. Soon, it led me to a radical plan to claim ultimate control over my longevity. But first, my financial advisor had my net worth burn rate verdict.

Using my current assets and diminished job related income (unless you tell lots of your friends to buy this book), my financial advisor determined that I could safely plan on living my current good life until—drum roll please—I am around 83. Really? Only 83? And I am considered a successful businessman who has planned for his retirement.

The planning session continued with building scenarios to get me past 83. Each required adjustments to how much money I have available, plan to earn and anticipate spending. Such modeling was all well and good, but it felt hollow since I had absolutely no way of factoring any true sense of my life expectancy into the equation in any meaningful way. This cognitive dissonance derailed the alleged premise that I could safely plan my future.

My disillusionment with conventional financial planning accelerated my radical thought exercise. I began to ask myself if it would be prudent to not leave my life expectancy to fate alone. After all, is fate the only recourse? And is longevity the only important variable that conventional wisdom tells us cannot be controlled?

What if I planned my life expectancy too? Wouldn't that improve the accuracy of my financial planning? I began to casually research what-if scenarios based on picking a date to die, a commitment date for a rational suicide. Choosing an end-date, a planned exit, a financial euthanasia or whatever one wants to call it, all of a sudden allowed me to create a credible financial plan based on facts, not fate. I could regain control… all good, right?

The New Age Of
Rational Suicide

Our culture has condemned suicide for generations. The concept of taking one's own life was first banned in religious treatises including the Bible and the Koran and further argued by religious theologians including St. Augustine in the sixth century. Suicide became a major mental health issue in the early 1900's with psychoanalysts including Sigmund Freud analyzing the suicidal mind. In the late 20th century, a national discussion about the legality and ethics of self-determined, physician-assisted suicide for the terminally ill arose thanks to modern medical advances in life-sustaining support and shifts in moral values.

The idea of rational suicide seems to be quite paradoxical. The majority of people believe that any thought of suicide must be associated with mental illness or a serious depression worthy of treatment. Therefore, the idea of "rational" cannot play a role in suicidal decision-making.

However, for many of us, accepting that someone with a painful terminal illness might seek a rational approach to ending life isn't that big of a leap. I'd like to think that the terminally ill's right to die when they want absolves them from being labeled mentally ill or out of touch with reality. Sadly, I'm not sure that this is the case as our legal system and theology currently trump personal decision-making.

Rational suicide is the concept that a sane person can make an objective decision about the benefits of ending one's life based on an assessment of his or her future. While generally associated with terminally ill patients, who in theory are simply ready to move past their daily pain, the concept of rational suicide is being discussed and considered by healthy people facing the uncertainties of aging. I am one of these people. As I conducted my research and discussed this book with both friends and new acquaintances, I learned that I am not alone in considering suicide as an option.

I see the tide shifting and fully agree with Margret P. Batten, professor of philosophy and ethics at the University of Utah, who states that rational suicide is, "an issue for the coming century" and "represents one of the fullest forms of expression of one's autonomy. It is the right of people to shape the ends of their lives." If you believe that the idea of self-determination is at the core of Baby Boomer psychology, then Ms. Batten's idea of self-expression must ring loud and clear. Rational suicide could be poised to become a big issue in this century.

The concept of choosing my end date was so obvious that I suspected that I couldn't be the only aging Baby Boomer contemplating rational suicide. It didn't take much research to validate my hypothesis. I am, in fact, not the only one convinced that a planned death makes sense. Further, it seems that almost everyone contemplating a rational suicide shares a related story; a story where they or a loved one had at least thought about the use of suicide as a sensible, methodical planning device. I was blown away by how deeply the idea resonated.

This book shares what I have learned about suicide; the often grisly statistics on violent suicide in America, the details about the rational suicide option in financial planning and, ultimately, my personal thoughts about the merits of taking control of life expectancy itself. This book also offers the prediction that, true to our generation, I might not be the only Baby Boomer thinking this way and that rational suicide will become part of the American conversation. We are, despite our desire to be individuals, very like-minded. Read on.

BABY BOOMERS: NOT AS GROOVY AS WE THOUGHT

National demographic trends show that the 48 to 64 year old Baby Boomers are committing suicide at an increasing, even alarming, rate.

According to the CDC's most recent study, the 45-64 age group had the highest suicide rate in 2009. From 2000 to 2009, the suicide rate for persons aged 45-64 years increased significantly from 13.2 to 17.6 per 100,000 in population. The rate for 55-64 increased by 4.6 points from 12.1 to 16.7. With more and more Boomers reaching 55+ every day, the math does not look very good for the aging Boomer population.

What's going on here?

As we all know, the stereotypical Baby Boomer is an over-pampered, well-educated, economically unencumbered and very entitled kid who grew up to be a flower-child, hippie, pot smoking anti-war protestor. Of course, like many stereotypes, ours probably doesn't reflect a universal reality but this has been a popular and conceptually simple, easy-to-digest image.

I have always been somewhat disheartened that this pampered Baby Boomer image has dogged us for years despite the fact that we have dutifully trudged off to our jobs, reinvented industries, raised super Gen-X and Y kids and are now caring for our aging parents. In fact, I bristle when I see Tom Brokaw's book The Greatest Generation. While the book is kind to our parents, it makes me ask what isn't to love about Baby Boomers? It is my sense that the "Greatest" are the enduring generation having lived through the depression and two wars. Our folks had to deal with tough times and successfully played the hand they were dealt. We, on the other hand, have been an action generation that challenges the status quo, believes deeply in personal choice, believes that the idea of change is good and delivers daily on the dream of the American Century. And, as they say in New Jersey, not f'nuthin, but we also had some unpleasant things to endure like Lawrence Welk, bellbottoms and Swanson TV dinners.

Stereotypes aside, what is unimpeachable is that we Baby Boomers share some significant events and trends.

The size of our generation coupled with a peacetime economy and our parent's spending habits (from cribs to suburban homes to station wagons) drove America's economic gain for years. We also grew up during a time of unprecedented social change: the lunar landings, the Cuban Missile crisis, the Civil Rights Movement, mass migration to the suburbs, the assassinations of JFK, RFK and MLK, drug experimentation, environmental awareness, the women's movement, bomb shelters, the Vietnam war, disposable income, the Mustang, VW Vans, Walter Cronkite, Ed Sullivan, the Beatles, Motown, Woodstock, Easy Rider, Steve McQueen, Elizabeth Taylor, go-go boots and mini-skirts, the pill, free-love, Playboy, transistor radios, color televisions, Steve Jobs, Nixon and Watergate and

Reagan. And in more recent history, our three Baby Boomer presidents: Clinton, Bush and Obama. I think that experiencing these very interesting times have encouraged us to think differently and make some of our unique lifestyle choices.

It should be noted that at 76 million strong, we are not a wholly homogenous group. With a wide 18-year age range, we are in different life-stages and have varying personal goals and needs. Leading Edge Boomers who were born between 1946 and1955 (Martin Gertler of the marketing company Boomerhead calls this the back 9) are potentially beyond their prime earning years whereas Trailing Edge Boomers born between 1956 and1964 (the front 9) are still earning, saving and raising children. Despite having achieved adulthood during the economic boom years of the 1960's through early 1980's, when GNP and personal incomes grew in the double-digits, we are also in a very wide range of income classes.

Looking at this generation as a whole, we expected to slowly move into the promised land of a secure, happy retirement. Unfortunately for many, this migration hasn't happened, isn't so secure and doesn't feel groovy. For some, if not many, it resulted in bad vibes.

Suicide research has revealed many factors that could be causing the increase in Baby Boomer suicides. Elevated pessimism about the future, a shared quality among Boomers, is one major factor worth considering. A 2010 study by the PEW Research Center reported that 21% of Boomers believe that their standard of living is lower than their parent's was at the same age, and 34% stated that their children will not share the same standard of living that they have.

Stop for a second and think about this increase in pessimism. True or not, just thinking that we did not live up to our dreams is significant. The idea that our prospects might not live up to our parent's retirement lifestyle and that our children's prospects could even be worse is emotionally demoralizing. This outcome was not in the Baby Boomer master playbook.

Since depression is a major cause of suicide, our generation's growing pessimism is almost certainly a factor in increased thoughts of suicide as a solution. Financial insecurity is not broken out in depression statistics but it goes to reason that money, or the lack of it, could play a large role in one's emotional state. This is especially true for Baby Boomers as we approach the end of our earning years. The negative effects of high unemployment and widespread ageism compound our mounting income anxieties. There is clearly a difference between clinical depression and anxiety but, the thought of having to say, "Welcome to Wal-Mart. Enjoy your shopping," or "Fries with that?" on a daily basis can be the stuff of nightmares.

Having to fight for those jobs is even scarier.

Socioeconomic statistics support the concept of rising financial depression. According to the 2011 Associated Press and LifeGoesStrong.com surveys, approximately 60% of Baby Boomers lost significant value in investments   due to t h e recent economic crisis, 42% are delaying retirement, and 25% claim they'll never retire and are currently working.

In respect to lost value, the Federal Reserve's 2012 Survey of Consumer Finances states that due to the ongoing economic downturn, the median American household has less wealth than it had in the 1990's. The study also shows a significant decrease in median net worth going from $126,400 in 2007 to $77,300 in 2010. These numbers may have increased since 2010, due to the rise in the stock market over the past couple of years.

But, our collective outlook is bleak. The Employee Benefit Retirement Research Institute reports that 52% of Americans believe that they will have a comfortable retirement.

These diminished prospects aren't what we expected as we marched to Woodstock. Dashed expectations, economic woes, depression or chronic medical problems may be factors in why the suicide rates for middle-aged Americans have increased. Tragically, those aren't the only variables that may be fueling the surge in suicides.

Divorce rates for couples over 50 have doubled in the past 20 years, according to a Bowling Green State University study. In 2009, one-in-four divorced couples was over 50. That same statistic in 1990 was one-in-ten. Now link that reality to the fact that married people live longer and you'll see the inconvenient truth. The American Journal of Epidemiology accentuated this conclusion when they reported that single people die a decade earlier than their married friends.

Americans are now living alone more than ever. Roughly 40% of all American households are single-person homes. Approximately 30% of adults aged 45-63 are unmarried. These statistics represent a greater than 50% increase since 1980.

Furthermore, our families are increasingly dispersed across America as many have moved to find jobs in more economically vibrant regions.

As a result of our migration, we have become increasingly disconnected from family and community support.

Many of these negative economic and societal factors have aligned to bring a degree of harsh reality to what was once a sense that the good life would just, as the Grateful Dead said, "keep on truckin." Well, since it won't, many of us are beginning to ask just what are some of our options?

Boomercide

You know the feeling that once you begin to pay attention to a particular word or subject you start to see it everywhere? While writing this book, I started to notice just how many newspapers, magazines and websites have started to talk about the looming issue of our retirement savings deficit. This is the one deficit that most Americans can truly understand and feel because it affects virtually every family. I wasn't even aware of this issue until I began to think through my own retirement and began to do my calculations.

Retirement savings deficit. It has a nasty ring to it. But, I am sure (or sure hope) that this emotionally charged subject is about to see even more discussion in the next couple of years as more Baby Boomers take a hard look at the fact that they haven't saved enough, by a long-shot, for retirement.

The numbers and implications are alarming. According to Retirement USA, the difference between what Americans will need for retirement and what they have actually saved is $6.6 trillion.

The Employee Benefit Research Institute reports on the average retirement savings of various age groups. The current figures are scary:

Workers ages 45-54 have saved just under $44,000.

Baby boomers, those aged 55-64, have approximately $65,000 in savings.

People 65+ have saved $56,000. If you retire at 65 and live to 85, that $56,000 doesn't go very far.

Scared yet? Here are four key facts that make me even more nervous (if one could even get more nervous.)

Retiring in some form is a given. A secure retirement is not. "Almost half of middle-class workers (49%) will be poor or near poor in retirement, living on a food budget of about $5 a day," according to Teresa Ghilarducci, professor of economics at the New School For Social Research.

The Fed isn't helping. Even if you have saved a decent nest egg, generating fixed income from savings is constrained by our historically low interest rates. As of fall 2012, a high yield money market account is yielding approximately .09%. 5-year certificates of deposit are running at approximately 1.75%. These low interest rates are racing neck and neck with inflation. We are at best breaking even.

Social Security won't save us. The average annual Social Security benefit for a retired worker is about $14,760 in 2012. This is perilously close to the individual poverty rate of $11,170 per year.

We could easily outlive our savings. The Social Security Administration reports that 25% of 65-year-olds will live past 90.

I find these facts beyond distressing. Worse, I find the fact that the great majority of our politicians are essentially ignoring this issue disgraceful. With such a obvious national problem about to explode – and keep exploding for more generations, it is nearly impossible to understand why Republicans rattle on about our $711 billion in military spending being too low and why Democrats can't engage in any intelligent review and national debate about our entitlements. Ignoring the retirement savings deficit issue is akin to across-the-board political malpractice.

Unless we start to bring the Baby Boomer retirement savings deficit problem out in the open, I anticipate that we are going to see an even higher incidence of depression resulting from personal financial deficits. This group malaise could potentially lead to an increase in suicides as the over 65-year-old group ages. To be clear, I think that adoption of the suicide option would be a result of two types of motivations.

Suicides motivated by depressive thoughts stemming from overwhelming financial instability, doubt, fear and resulting emotional pain.

Rational suicides from strategic life-expectancy-based financial planning.

I call this Boomercide. I am not an economist, psychologist or suicideologist. However, I studied math. With Baby Boomer suicide rates and population already on the rise, it is reasonable to imagine that we will see even more suicides.

If there is any possible good news in what could become a devastating trend, it is that we should begin to see a more aggressive public discussion about the retirement savings issue.

It may be too late for many Baby Boomers to change our savings habits but, hopefully, not our kids.

To reverse the course of our savings debacle, it must be made crystal clear that our nation, especially the young who have time, must rethink our approach to saving for retirement.

The current self-directed system that includes 401Ks isn't working. Today, less than half of private sector workers are covered by employer-sponsored pension or retirement plans. Even public workers, who once viewed their pensions as sacrosanct, must now live in fear of the $1.38 billion shortfall in state retirement systems. According to Michael Calabrese of the New America Foundation in his 2012 testimony before the US Senate, "Most individuals are simply not saving enough over their working life to supplement the meager benefits they will receive from Social Security."

As we become more aware of the retirement savings deficit and what I think will be an inevitable increase in Baby Boomer suicides, we will be forced to take a closer look at the act of suicide itself. We will see the press move from reporting on the latest celebrity suicide to a deeper review of all the factors that drive our neighbors to consider ending their lives.

I admit that understanding the why and how of suicide became more important to me as the prospect of my own suicide was becoming more real. To put it mildly, I became very curious about the details.

Suicide: The Details

As I began to imagine taking my own life, I realized that I knew very little about suicide beyond the occasional celebrity suicide story. I needed to get a better understanding of the facts and about the act itself. I became one of the millions who search online for information on the subject of suicide and quickly discovered that in-depth discussions of suicide and specific how-to instructions are readily available.

How many do it?

Approximately 100 Americans take their own life very day, equating to about one suicide every 15 minutes. According to the CDC, 36,909 suicide deaths were reported in the U.S. in 2009 (the CDC's latest reporting year). This represents a statistically significant 4% increase over 2008.

While 36,909 is a large number, it is dwarfed by the approximately 8 to 25 attempted suicides for every successful suicide. That means that the incidence of suicide attempts could be close to one million every year and these are only the attempts we know about.

Who does it?

- Men complete suicide 3.7 times more than women.
- Women attempt suicide 3 times more than men.
- White males 65+ have the highest suicide rate. But according to demographic trends, Baby Boomers are not alone in contemplating suicide.
- Suicide is the third leading cause of death for young people aged 15-24 year olds and the second leading cause of death for 25-34 year olds.
- African Americans have a significantly lower suicide rate than the national average, and black females have the lowest rate for all ages combined.

According to the U.S. Army's report, Generating Health and Discipline in the Force Ahead of the Strategic Reset, active-duty service members have an alarming suicide rate. Presently, approximately one active-duty military suicide occurs per day. This number far surpasses the U.S. forces killed in action in Afghanistan—about 50% more—according to Pentagon statistics.

Not surprisingly, the press picked up on the military's easy to digest once-per-day suicide sound-bite and it became a big story. TIME Magazine did a masterful job of reporting on this in its July 23, 2012 cover story One A Day. Two of the most painful realities are that 95% of military suicides take place on U.S. soil and that our government hasn't allocated the funds necessary to provide adequate mental health care for our soldiers. Evidently, protecting our military's mental health isn't as attractive to Congress as building new $113 million F-35 fighter jets. Just one less F-35 could easily pay for better and timelier mental health counseling for our military personnel. The Department of Veteran Affairs says that we need 20% more psychiatrists at our VA hospitals. USA Today reports that, "The VA needed to hire 266 psychiatrists last September (2011) and it was taking an average of eight months to fill each job…"

And then there are dentists.

Is the common belief that dentistry is the most suicide prone profession in the U.S. true? Well, it's close enough that if I were graduating from Oregon's OHSU School of Dentistry, I wouldn't be heading to live in Montana—the state with the highest suicide rate. This particular combination doesn't instill a sense of long-term employment.

What other professions have high suicide rates? Definitive answers are hard to come by, as many states do not track the occupations of suicide victims. However, a list of the top white male professions that have committed suicide from the National Institute for Occupational Safety and Health offers some guidance. High stress engineers, financiers, lawyers and, most interestingly, a range of healthcare professionals including veterinarians make the list.

The top 10 suicide-prone professions:

1. Marine engineers (strange, right?)
2. Physicians
3. Dentists
4. Veterinarians
5. Finance workers
6. Chiropractors

7. Supervisors of heavy construction equipment

8. Real estate agents

9. Electrical equipment assemblers

10. Lawyers

And at number 13, Pharmacists...

Why do so many healthcare professionals commit suicide? Doctors alone have a suicide rate almost twice as high as the general population. Experts point to the fact that the medical industry has access to lethal drugs and the knowledge of how to administer them. Medical professionals are the only group that use drug overdoses at a higher rate than firearms. Interestingly, and counter to national averages, male and female doctors have the same rate of suicide.

There are other factors that may be causing medical profession suicides. Seeking mental health counseling is likely difficult for doctors who need to protect their professional reputations. High financial debt is another factor; average debt for graduating medical students in 2009 was $156,000. Tension from an insurance dominated industry and the stress of dealing with increasing numbers of patients per day are other probable factors.

Why they do it?

While we can't ask the successful for their reasons, we can make reasonable deductions based on our knowledge of the mental state and circumstances of people who have committed suicide. We also have insight into the mind-set of people who have had unsuccessful suicide attempts.

Not surprisingly, according to research by organizations like the CDC and the National Institute of Mental Health, mental and/or emotional disorders are believed to be the primary causes of suicide.

The primary risk factors for suicide include:

- Depression and other mental ailments.
- Substance abuse (often in combination with mental disorders.)
- Exposure to the suicidal behavior of others, such as family members, peers, or media figures.
- A family history of mental disorders, substance abuse and family violence.
- Incarceration.
- Firearms in the home (the method used in more than half of suicides.)

Biochemistry may also play a role. Postmortem studies of suicide victim's brains have indicated that the risk of suicide might be caused by a chemical imbalance. Low levels of a serotonin metabolite, the product produced by the breakdown of serotonin, are considered by some to be a cause of elevated states of depression and have been detected in the spinal fluid of persons who have attempted suicide.

A personal sense of situational hopelessness where there is no sense of improvement in one's circumstances may be a growing cause of suicide. This shouldn't be surprising given today's depressed economic environment and group-malaise where many of us wonder how, or if, we will ever regain our personal and societal optimism.

Beyond healthcare, there are other profession-specific factors that drive suicides. A famous subset includes recent suicides by ex-NFL football players. Suicides by Junior Seau of the Chargers, Andre Waters of the Eagles, and Terry Long of the Steelers indicate that there may be an emerging pattern of suicides based on the long-term effects of repeated brain injury from playing football. The Bears' Dave Duerson, who shot himself in the chest, wrote a note asking that his brain be donated to science. It was his wish that his brain be used to study the long-term effects of concussions and other football-related brain injuries.

How do they do it?

The method used in premeditated suicide is a very personal decision. Based on my research and personal rationale, this choice is generally driven by a decision making process that considers one or more of the following factors:

Success Rate

Gunshots are by far the most popular form of suicide in the United States at 53.7% of all suicides, according to the American Association of Suicidology. Firearms are incredibly efficient and effective unless your aim is poor or you select a small caliber bullet. Firearms are followed by drug and alcohol overdoses, suffocation (hanging and carbon monoxide inhalation) and poisoning.

Availability

Suicide rates are highest in states with high firearm ownership. Likewise, drug overdoses are high in states where access to pharmaceuticals has been easier (think Florida's "pill-mills".) And the Golden Gate Bridge accounts for approximately 40% of suicides among citizens of Marin County, which is just north of the bridge. Proximity matters.

Ease

Easy to obtain and use methods, like drugs and firearms, allow the act to be completed with minimal operational difficulty.

Degree of Pain

Drug overdoses and helium inhalation are perceived to be relatively painless. By contrast, electrocution, poisoning and bleeding out are particularly painful methods.

Consideration for others

While suicide has not been generally associated with rational decision-making, many people do consider the effect that the physical nature of their suicide will have on the people left behind. Some forms of suicide are particularly violent, messy and disturbing. Ernest Hemingway was particularly inconsiderate, if not insane, at the time of his death. According to Hemingway's biographer Michael S. Reynolds, Hemmingway put the barrel of his 12-guage shotgun in his mouth and pulled the trigger. He performed this act in his front foyer while his wife was in another room.

Consideration for others also results in using methods that might look like an accident to family, friends, doctors and the law. Drowning and car-related suicides are often reported as accidents.

The Popular Methods

Suicide methods vary by sex. For men, suicide by firearm is most common, followed by suffocation, hanging and poisoning. Women choose poisoning followed by firearms, suffocation and hanging. Generally speaking, the most prevalent methods include:

Firearms

As mentioned earlier, firearms are the most common suicide method in America, accounting for over 50% of all suicides. The majority use firearms at close range aimed at the head. With a success rate of 99%, a headshot is the most typical form of firearm-based suicide. A chest shot ranks second, but for obvious reasons, mostly related to poor aim, there is greater room for error. Interestingly, those retired NFL football players that commit suicide appear to favor self-inflicted chest shots because they want to donate their brains to research.

The caliber of firearm is very important. The relatively small .22 caliber gun results in a lower success rate than shotguns and higher caliber pistols. Often, hollow point bullets are used to maximize tissue damage to increase the success rate.

Suffocation and Asphyxiation

Suffocation leads to asphyxia and hypoxia (lack of oxygen.). Suffocation can be achieved via placing a bag over one's head or by confinement in a closed-in space to reduce oxygen intake. Depressants are often employed in the act of suffocation to allow the individual to die from oxygen deprivation before they experience panic.

The inhalation of high levels of carbon monoxide (an odorless and colorless gas) also leads to a relatively painless death. Famous for its association with automobiles, hoses and garages, the inhalation of high levels of carbon monoxide leads to death by hypoxia. Carbon monoxide deaths are often done in enclosed spaces like cars and garages.

Death from charcoal burning is believed to be effective when the burner is placed in an enclosed space leading to carbon monoxide poisoning. This method gained widespread popularity in Japan in the mid-2000's and was known as "hibachi" suicides.

Helium hoods are a growing method of asphyxiation. Helium can be self-administered, is painless and is considered highly efficient. The method usually consists of a large plastic bag connected to one or two helium tanks. The bag is placed over the head and the helium is pumped into the bag via a tube for inhalation. Death occurs from oxygen deprivation. Helium and helium hood-kits can be purchased legally. There are exit-bag retailers, albeit a somewhat shady bunch, that sell their equipment on the Internet.

This method gained broad international awareness due to Derek Humphry's best-selling books on suicide, Final Exit and How To Make Your Own Helium Hood Kit. In fact, a friend's retired parent in Florida recently went to what she described as a well-attended but secret seminar for seniors on the use of helium hoods. I am still trying to visualize people going to the seminar and then trying to make the early bird happy hour at the local diner.

On a somewhat lighter side, after I mentioned the helium option to a friend she told me that she will never be able to look at birthday balloons the same way again. Oops.

Hanging

Hanging results in strangulation and/or a broken neck. The length of the rope and the distance of the fall determine the actual cause of death. Short-drops generally lead to strangulation and long-drops lead to fractures of the cervical vertebrae. Like death by firearm, hanging is a violent end that can have a devastating effect on people finding and dealing with the aftermath.

Poisoning

Death from poisoning is achieved by consuming substances like household cleaners, industrial fluids and even poisonous plants. Fast-acting chemicals like hydrogen cyanide (Prussic acid) have become famous in literature and movies including the James Bond books where double-0 agents were given a cyanide capsule to bite in case of capture. The use of cyanide is low as it is difficult to purchase potassium cyanide. Pesticides are used in countries with large farming populations where access to these chemicals is common.

Poisoning is viewed as a highly unreliable method since it is difficult to determine the correct amount of poison and failure can lead to significant pain and long-term injury.

Jumping

Despite the fame of the Golden Gate Bridge, jumping is not a favorite means of suicide. Leaps of death account for less than 2% of suicide deaths in the United States. However, jumping accounts for over 50% of suicides in Hong Kong, possibly due to the number of tall buildings and strong gun-control laws.

As is the case with many suicide techniques, failure from jumping can have nasty consequences including broken bones, internal injuries and paralysis.

Drug Overdose

Modern society's access to pharmaceutical drugs has increased the incidence of fatal drug overdoses. Additionally, the planned use of drug overdoses in physician-assisted suicides has become one of the preferred methods of dignified dying, where legal.

Given the complexity of taking the correct dose of the right drugs, the failure rate of drug overdoes is high. Often, people vomit before the drug can take effect. Therefore many who select drug overdose as their suicide method also take antiemetics to prevent vomiting.

Common suicide drugs include barbiturates such as Seconal and Nembutal and Diazepam (i.e. Valium) taken with alcohol, opiates or other depressants. Toxicity can be increased by as much as 50% when the drugs are taken with alcohol.

These drugs have become more difficult to obtain legally. However, the growing illegal international pharmaceutical drug trade may be helping to make these drugs and other drugs like pentobarbital more available for resourceful shoppers.

People also make deadly cocktails of over-the-counter drugs, including analgesics. But the failure rate of such home-made mixtures is high and can lead to severe internal organ damage.

Cutting and Piercing

Known in Japan as Jigai for women and Seppuku for men, exsanguination (or cutting to induce bleeding) results in massive blood loss. This method has become popular for teenagers in western countries.

Cutting, even slitting the wrist, has a low success rate. To increase effectiveness, wrist cutting needs to be performed vertically along the vein rather than across it. Especially for younger demographics, cutting can be a form of parasuicide, an attempt where death is not the desired outcome.

Drowning

Drowning is simply submerging and suffocating in water or another liquid. The efficiency of drowning can be increased by submersion in very cold water. Because our bodies are built with a primal need to breathe, drowning requires planning. People often add weight to their bodies to counter act this natural reflex. Famously, Virginia Woolf added stones to her coat pockets before drowning herself in a river.

Drowning is the third leading cause of unintentional, injury-based death worldwide. For this reason, people who want their suicide to look like an accident often choose drowning.

Vehicular

The two most common types of vehicular suicide are the use of cars and trains.

In vehicular impact suicide, a people places themself, either alone or in a vehicle, in the path of a large and fast-moving vehicle. Suicide by train impact results in an approximately 90% death rate.

Death by automotive collision is deliberate and often done by single drivers in single vehicle crashes. Due to the nature of the act, suicide from a deliberate crash can be more spontaneous than other methods of suicide. Many believe this type of suicide is advantageous in that the crash may look like an accident to families and the police, especially when there is no suicide note. Because of this, the incidence of pre-meditated automotive suicides is most likely under-reported.

Electric Shock

One of the most painful ways to commit suicide is through the use of lethal electric shock. The shock causes the heart to fail triggering a reduction of blood flow. This method requires ample electrical engineering awareness, thus resulting in a high degree of failure. Perhaps electric shock is better left up to the warden.

Buy a Cat

As I write this, many news organizations across the globe are reporting that women who own cats might have higher suicide rates than those who live in non-cat households. The reports are based on a study in the July 2012 issue of Archives of General Psychiatry that found that a percentage of women who have been infected with the Toxoplasma gondii parasite found in some cats' feces have a 150% higher chance of committing suicide than those that were not infected.

The press loved this "lighter" view of suicide and delivered somewhat alarmist "Cat" headlines:

- "'Cat ladies' more likely to commit suicide, scientists claim", (The Telegraph)
- "Common parasite found in cat litter may increase suicide risk", (FOX News)
- "Kitty litter may potentially increase suicide risk", (NY Daily News)

While attention grabbing, these findings have been overstated by the press. The fact is that while exposure to Toxoplasma gondii can somewhat increase the desire to self-harm—especially in pregnant women—this parasite is also found in unwashed vegetables, undercooked meat and contaminated water.

Where do they do it?

According to the CDC, the incidence of American suicides is highest in the inter-mountain states of Montana, Alaska, Wyoming, Idaho, Nevada, New Mexico, Colorado, Arizona and Utah.

Why these western states? Could their residents be more depressed than the national average? Are these westerners more isolated? Are they less religious? Do they have a greater sense of individualism and a Libertarian outlook?

As a western state resident, I am well aware that my neighbors exhibit a greater degree of self-sufficiency and a residual "cowboy" or "pioneer" mentality. We have a tendency toward being more private about our situation and feelings. Could this western lifestyle and culture play a role in the desire to take charge of one's demise?

Regardless of any cultural propensity toward self-determination, a western state resident's easy access to firearms dramatically increases the chance for a successful suicide for anyone considering the act. The statistics are clear: mountain state residents have much greater access to the ultimate suicide method of choice. Guns are efficient; the success rate is high. The correlation between access to guns and a high suicide rate, while not definitive, seems obvious based on research.

In 2001, the Behavioral Risk Factor Surveillance System in North Carolina surveyed 201,881 respondents nationwide, asking them, "Are any firearms now kept in or around your home? Include those kept in a garage, outdoor storage area, car, truck, or other motor vehicle." According to the survey, Wyoming (at 59.7% ownership), Alaska (57.8%), Montana (57.7%), Idaho (55.3%) and Utah (43.9%) are leading gun ownership states, and, not surprisingly, the leading suicide states.

In contrast, high population northeast states with strict gun laws have lower suicide rates. The District of Columbia has only 3.8% gun ownership and the lowest suicide rate in the U.S. New Jersey has the second lowest suicide rate with 12.3% gun ownership.

Because of the power of the National Rifle Association (NRA) to influence our national gun laws, I researched their perspective on gun ownership and suicide. One of the issues de jour is the NRA's attack on the Department of Veterans Affairs' (VA) pamphlet Firearms and Dementia. The NRA finds fault with much, if not all, of the VA's firearm awareness message, which states, "The presence of firearms in households has been linked to increased risk of injury or death for everyone in or around the home," and "Firearms in the home can in-crease the possibility of completing suicide." It makes sense for military counselors to talk to at-risk active-duty soldiers about owning a gun, right? Um, no if you are the NRA. Rather than intelligently dealing with the important issue of gun re-lated suicides in the military, the gun lobby decries the VA pamphlet as "what the taxpayers get when people who know nothing about firearms issues take their cues from people who lie about firearms issues."

Keep the NRA's position in mind while thinking about the increase in military suicides.

Wondering if there is a similar correlation between gun ownership and homicide rates? There is. According to the study *Rates of Household Firearm Ownership and Homicide Across US Regions and States, 1988–1997* (Harvard School of Public Health), "Although our study cannot determine causa-tion, we found that in areas where household firearm owner-ship rates were higher, a disproportionately large number of people died from homicide."

Happy Places

One might assume that there is a correlation between a coun-try's collective happiness and its suicide rates. This may be the case in Greece in 2012 where the suicide rate has close to doubled due in part to the current economic malaise con-fronting the Greek economy. Greece used to have one of the lowest suicide rates in Europe.

To see if there is actually a correlation between happy and unhappy countries and their suicide rates, I read Eric Weiner's book *The Geography of Bliss: One Grump's Search for the Happiest Places in the World.* Weiner cites Bhutan as the happiest place on earth with its concept of Gross National Happiness and Eastern Europe's Moldova as the unhappiest.

Unfortunately, Bhutan is not ranked on the World Health Organization (WHO) suicide by country list so we can't relate its mood to suicidal behavior. But Moldova is ranked by WHO and appears in the top 20 countries for suicides. Other post-Communist countries match the Moldavian's relative propensity for suicidal behavior. Russia and other former Soviet Union countries, including Lithuania (42 suicides per 100,000), Russia (38), Belarus (35) and Ukraine (26) have high suicide rates. Even Hungary has a high rate (27) possibly because of its long history of occupation by Soviet masters.

This happiness-to-suicide trend made great sense to me until I noted that the generally happy populations of Sweden and Denmark have relatively high suicide rates. They are ranked at 30 and 35 respectively out of the top 107 countries on the list. Possibly, their rates are high due to having very short, dark, gloomy winter months.

My happy-to-unhappy formula became further confused when I discovered the findings from Dark Contrasts: The paradox of high rates of suicide in happy places that ran in the December 2011 Journal of Economic Behavior & Organization. The report concludes that despite living in a happy place, it might be particularly, even intensely, painful to be unhappy if one is surrounded by very happy people.

The researchers cited Utah, which is ranked 1st in happiness and life satisfaction yet 9th in highest U.S. suicide rate, as corroborating evidence of this finding.

Conversely, New York State, which despite ranking very low in happiness at the 45th position has the second lowest suicide rate in the U.S. It would seem that collective unhappiness might actually be a good way to reduce suicide rates, a confusing finding when you think about the joys of living in Moldova.

There is another place that is at the intersection of joy and sadness and is known around the world for its suicides.

The Bridge

More people commit suicide from the Golden Gate Bridge than from any other single location. Anywhere.

Researchers estimate that over 1,500 people have jumped off the bridge since it opened in 1937. That number has been slowly increasing in recent years. Thirty-seven people died jumping from the bridge in 2011, and at least 100 were dissuaded from jumping by bridge authorities and bystanders.

Who jumps from the bridge? According to the San Francisco Chronicle, "Three to one, they're men, according to a recent study by the Psychiatric Foundation of Northern California that compiled Marin County coroner's reports from January 1995 to July 2005. Eighty-seven percent are Bay Area residents—exploding the myth that people flock from around the world to die here." Approximately 40% of all Marin County, CA suicides take place on the bridge. In fact, only 5% of jumpers in the 1995–2005 period were non-Californians.

Additional reporting from the Marin County Coroners Office reports that the majority of bridge suicides were male (74%) and white (82%).

Ages ranged from 14 to 85 with a median of 40. Overall, 55% had never married, 23% were divorced and 21% were married.

Why this bridge? It appears to be a combination of ease, efficiency and emotion. Unlike many other bridges, the Golden Gate has a pedestrian walkway with a railing height of only 4 feet and no suicide barrier. At 245 feet (75m), a jump from the bridge has a 98% success rate. A jumper will hit the water after the four-second fall at a velocity of 75 MPH (120km/hr). When you consider that hitting water at that speed is like hitting concrete, it is clear that the bridge is a highly effective suicide device.

Beyond simply viewing the bridge as an available and effective tool, there is an element of romance surrounding the Golden Gate Bridge due to its location, fame and history.

Over the years, the Golden Gate Bridge has stared in many movies including *Dirty Harry*, *A View To Kill* and *X-Men*. But possibly the most riveting Golden gate movie is the documentary The Bridge. Eric Steel and his crew focused their cameras on the bridge for one year and captured 23-suicide jumps along with the personal stories of the jumpers. The film received critical acclaim including this from Stephen Holden's review in *The New York Times*, "'The Bridge' juxtaposes breathtaking scenes of the Golden Gate and its environs, shot in digital video, with the harrowing personal stories of family members and friends of those who jumped. Because their testimony is remarkably free of religious cant and of cozy New Age bromides, this is one of the most moving and brutally honest films about suicide ever made."

The movie has helped to highlight the Golden Gate Bridge

as one of the few destination bridges that does not have any suicide prevention netting.

Why not? The combination of high cost (estimated at $50 million), aesthetics (some want to keep the world's most beautiful bridge as is) and a sense of west coast Libertarianism (which suggests that it is an individual's right to act on her desires without government intervention) has outweighed calls for a preventative barrier.

Failure:
Success is Not Guaranteed
(Or Always Desired)

The great majority of suicide attempts fail. While statistics vary due to the difficulty of tracking, it is generally believed that there are as high as 30 suicide attempts for every success. Reports show that over 2 million adult Americans make plans to commit suicide annually.

As you could imagine, many people consider suicide and never make any plans. SAMHSA's 2009 National Survey on Drug Use and Health reports "Nearly 8.3 million adults age 18 and older in the United States (3.7%) had serious thoughts of suicide in the past year." Despite the ease of talking about suicide, suicide experts urge us to pay close attention to any mention of the act – especially from children and teens.

Women attempt suicide two to three times more often than men, but they are three times more likely to be unsuccessful. Age also makes a difference in number of attempts. Younger women make many more attempts than younger men, whereas women older than 50 make slightly fewer attempts than men.

Failed suicides can be attributed to a very dramatic cry for help, which in some cases can result in a much-improved life. The 2002 study "The Economics of Suicide" by Dave Marcotte of the University of Maryland, found that suicide failures could lead to an income increase of 20.6%. "Hard-suicide", defined as an attempt that is more serious in nature, could increase income by as much as 36.3%. Why? These failures often lead to improved medical and psychiatric care, counseling and increased family attention. It is possible that many failed suicides are actually a form of rational choice for people calling out for much needed attention.

Additional reasons for failure include the desire to hurt third parties (as in friends, relatives and care givers), a sudden change of heart and/or a simple failure in technique. Some suicide techniques have much higher rates of failure than others. As discussed earlier, wrist cutting and drug overdoses have a much higher failure rate than use of guns. Guns work.

One would hope that suicide failure is a result of someone seeking help rather than poor planning as failure often leads to significant pain and serious injury.

A sound way to insure that you will actually succeed is to enlist the help of your doctor. As you'll see, this is easy for me to say

Physician-Assisted Suicide: Coming To A Neighborhood Near You

Do we have the right to end our own lives?

A 2009 CBS News public opinion survey found that Americans are evenly split when asked, "Should physician-assisted suicide be allowed?" As you might expect, 66% of those who attend religious services weekly or near weekly most strongly oppose physician-assisted suicide. By contrast, 60% of liberals and Northeasterners think physician-assisted suicide should be allowed. In the more recent May 2012 study conducted by The Polling Institute at Western New England University, it was confirmed that 60% of Massachusetts voters support "allowing people who are dying to legally obtain medication that they could use to end their lives."

Polls aside, and assuming you are a sane being, is the choice of physician-assisted suicide really anyone's business but yours? Apparently it is if you don't live in Oregon or Washington, the only states that respect the individual's right to decide how and when to die.

The good news for me is that I do live in Oregon. Oregon respects my right to choose when to die and the state's 1997 Death With Dignity Act made this right legal. As a Oregon resident, if I have a physician confirmed illness with six months or less to live and if I can convince the government of my sanity, I can request that a physician prescribe life-ending medicine as long as it is self-administered. The method of choice is a barbiturate cocktail created by a local pharmacy. Our assisted-suicide law was upheld in Gonzales v. Oregon, a United States Supreme Court decision that ruled that the United States Attorney General could not enforce the federal Controlled Substances Act against Oregon physicians who prescribed life-ending drugs. Close to 600 Oregonians have chosen death with dignity.

New Yorkers, for example, aren't afforded that same right. Somehow, using our nation's convoluted legal logic, a terminally ill New Yorker living with debilitating pain doesn't have the right to choose when to die. New York and 47 other states mandate that you live in pain without any hope, choice or self-determination.

Euthanasia isn't legal anywhere. There's an important distinction between physician-assisted suicide and euthanasia. In physician-assisted suicide, a doctor provides the means of suicide to the patient and the patient performs the act. The patient consciously kills him/herself. If a physician or another person actually delivers the means of death, it is considered euthanasia, which is illegal in all 50 states.

Sadly, our society allows us to provide a caring means of ending life for our sick dogs and cats but not our family or friends. This rather contradictory situation has been driven by physicians' narrow view of their "do no harm" mission, religious groups (is there no heaven for Fido?) and deeply entrenched moral beliefs. For a detailed perspective on the views of the clergy, read the Catholic Archdiocese of Boston's statement *Suicide Is Always A Tragedy*.

Dr. Death

Dr. Jack Kevorkian, the most famous (or infamous) proponent of physician-assisted suicide completed his first assisted-suicide in Michigan in 1990. Janet Adkins, a 54-year-old Oregon woman diagnosed in 1989 with Alzheimer's, was his first patient. Because no hospital would provide a safe place for Mrs. Adkin's injection, Kevorkian had to perform the act in his Volkswagen bus.

Dr. Kevorkian's Thanatron suicide machine allowed patients to self-administer a sixty-second IV drip of thiopental—a barbiturate general anesthetic. The patient then slipped quickly into a coma. The Thanatron next administered a lethal dose of potassium chloride to stop the heart. (Potassium chloride is the same chemical used in lethal death-penalty injections.) In 1991 Michigan's state Board of Medicine revoked his medical license. After that he was unable to purchase the drugs so he helped to administer a lethal dose of carbon monoxide via his Mercitron device.

Due to his relentless advocacy and sensational national press, Dr. Kevorkian became a global voice for assisted-suicide. Over an eight-year span, he performed 130 assisted suicides. After he lost his license, he was prosecuted in four murder cases that ended in either acquittal or a mistrial. Our society's fear and distaste for the idea of physician-assisted suicide finally caught up with Dr. Kevorkian. In 1998, he was found guilty of second-degree murder in a case where he had personally administered the lethal drugs and he spent 8 years in prison.

Dr. Kevorkian died in 2011. His New York Times obituary on June 3, 2011 read, "In arguing for the right of the terminally ill to choose how they die, Dr. Kevorkian challenged social taboos about disease and dying while defying prosecutors and the courts. He spent eight years in prison after being convicted of second-degree murder in the death of the last of about 130 ailing patients, whose lives he had helped end."

"The doctor's critics were as impassioned as his supporters, but all generally agreed that his stubborn and often intemperate advocacy of assisted suicide helped spur the growth of hospice care in the United States and made many doctors more sympathetic to those in severe pain and more willing to prescribe medication to relieve it."

As Dr. Kevorkian stated the day after his first assisted-suicide, "My ultimate aim is to make euthanasia a positive experience…I'm trying to knock the medical profession into accepting its responsibilities, and those responsibilities include assisting their patients with death."

The subject of assisted-suicide is clearly fraught with moral, religious and legal questions. But, at the end of the day, why is how I want to end my life anyone's business but my family's and mine? As I write this, a British Columbia Supreme Court judge has declared Canada's laws against physician-assisted suicide unconstitutional because they discriminate against the physically disabled. Telling me that I can't choose to die, whether I am disabled or not, seems discriminatory as well.

Ta Da—Sayonara— Finis—The End

I know, I know. It's an obvious title for the last chapter of a book about suicide, and yet it is so perfectly appropriate I couldn't help myself. So what have I decided?

I'll start with an easy decision. I am never, ever going to allow my body to end up in any form of a vegetative state. Likewise, I will never live in unbearable pain due to the miraculous advances of medical science and/or the desire of doctors to keep me alive despite my own wishes. I will also be very clear in my communications with my family about my end-of-life wishes and will make sure that all of the legal bows are tied.

To understand the importance of creating the right legal documentation, all we need to do is remember Terry Schiavo and the 15 years from 1990 to 2005 that she lived in a vegetative state while her husband and parents argued with each other and state and federal authorities over her right to die. Despite widespread political intervention, a ABC poll showed that 70 percent of Americans believed Congressional and White House involvement were inappropriate in the saga. Schiavo died after her feeding tube was finally removed.

She passed away 13 days later.

To ensure that my wishes are met, I have enacted a seven-point plan starting with legally sound, crystal-clear advance directives.

The Legal Loose Ends

1. Advance Directives: Living Will and Durable Power Of Attorney

My living will includes an advance directive, which is a legal document that specifies my decisions about end-of-life care. It is designed to eliminate any confusion for my family, friends, lawyers and healthcare professionals about my end-of-life choices. I view this document as essential as having a will.

Considering the emotional and financial issues associated with long-term illness, I do not understand why creating a living will remains so difficult for people. A 2012 study from the California Health Foundation says that 60% of people claim that making sure their family is not burdened by tough decisions is "extremely important" yet 56% have not communicated their end-of-life wishes. I suggest that you visit the informative website of the Conversation Project to learn more about how to have end-of-life conversations. As more and more of us Baby Boomers age, this conversation must be had.

Another legal document, my durable power of attorney, names my wife as my healthcare proxy. She is now empowered to make healthcare decisions for me should I be unable to do so myself. The durable power of attorney only works for the cessation of treatment. My wife cannot ask a doctor to end my life through an active form of euthanasia—only I can do that. I have made these important restrictions clear to her in case she gets any big ideas, if you know what I mean.

2. My Will

To grant peace of mind to my family and myself and to remove any probate issues, I have an up-to-date will. My will names my wife or, should her death precede mine, my adult children as manager of my estate including the transfer of property upon my death. It is hard to imagine that approximately 50% of Americans do not have up-to-date wills.

To set up the advance directives and a will, I recommend that you consult your attorney or do as I did and use the on-line services of Legalzoom. Legalzoom was once a client of my advertising agency; I know them to be smart, professional, helpful, fast and affordable. I have been using their services for years.

3. Social Security Entitlements and Retirement Savings

I made sure that I understood the nuances of the timing of Social Security entitlements and retirement savings distributions.

The age at which you begin to receive Social Security payments will determine your monthly benefit. To be very clear on this point, here is how the Social Security Administration describes this on their website:

"Let's say your full retirement age is 66 and your monthly benefit starting at that age is $1,000. If you choose to start getting benefits at age 62, your monthly benefit will be reduced by 25 percent to $750 to account for the longer period of time you receive benefits. This is generally a permanent reduction in your monthly benefit.

If you choose to not receive benefits until age 70, you would increase your monthly benefit amount to $1,320."

Second, in most cases, if you withdraw money from an IRA, 401(k) or pension plan before age 59 1/2, you have to pay a 10% penalty on top of ordinary income taxes. Before you begin to make any such withdrawals you should review the current laws and consult with a financial advisor.

4. Oregon Residency

I will maintain my Oregon residency since Oregon is one of the two states (Washington is the other) to have liberal physician-assisted suicide laws. It's worth noting, however, that bills supporting physician-assisted suicide have been proposed in Hawaii, Massachusetts, Montana, New York and Pennsylvania. I am sure that the subject of physician-assisted suicide will continue to resonate and possibly lead to new laws as our population grows older and lengthy terminal illnesses become even more commonplace.

5. Life Insurance

I first purchased life insurance when my children were very young to ensure that my family would be taken care of if I died. If you have family that depends on your work, I recommend that you get term life insurance. Sign up sooner than later because the older you are, the more expensive life insurance gets.

One of the most common questions I've been asked about suicide concerns life insurance, specifically whether or not a policy pays death benefits if the policyholder commits suicide. The general answer is yes, the policy will pay, but the policy most likely includes a restrictive suicide clause. The clause usually states that the insurer will not pay if one commits suicide within the first two years of the policy.

Every policy has its own legal language so pay close attention to your policy's exclusions section. Here are sample clauses from two different policies as examples:

Sample Policy #1

We will limit the proceeds we pay under this policy if the insured commits suicide, while sane or insane:

1. within two years from the earlier of the Date of Issue or the Policy date; or

2. after two years from earlier of the Date of issue or Policy date, but within two years from the effective date of the last reinstatement of this policy.

If 1 applies, the limited amount will equal all premiums paid on this policy.

If 2 applies, the limited amount will be all premiums paid on this policy on and after the effective date of the last reinstatement of this policy.

Sample Policy #2

The benefits payable are limited if the insured commits suicide, while sane or insane, within two years from the Issue Date. In such case, our liability will be limited to a refund of all premiums paid to us.

Note that there is often an exception to the two-year clause for employer-provided group insurance.

Despite the universal belief in the value of life insurance, the number of Americans with life insurance is now at the lowest level in 50 years.

Need cash now? You can cash in your life insurance policy before you die. There is a burgeoning industry dedicated to matching the terminally ill and their life insurance policies with investors looking for an investment. The investor pays the insured a portion of the death benefit upfront for the right to be their beneficiary at their death. Companies like The Lifeline Program will help you cash in. To see how mainstream the life-settlement business has become, check out Betty White's "I'm still hot" rap video on YouTube that was sponsored by The Lifeline Program.

6. My DNR Tattoo

While the TV show Portlandia has exaggerated many aspects of living in Portland, it is accurate in its portrayal of the heavily inked under 30 Portlander. I am no longer surprised by the plethora of tattoos and continue to be amazed at the growth and variety of this form of self-expression. In fact, I was so inspired by the artistry that I decided it was time to get inked too. In honor of this book and to support the decisions made in my advance directive, I had *do not resuscitate* tattooed on my left forearm. I consider the tattoo a visual advance directive that is carried on my person at all times. It may even help me to sell more books as it has already sparked many random conversations. Interestingly, my tattoo artist told me that the only other people that have asked for a DNR tattoos are in healthcare. What do they know that we don't?

These are the easy decisions. Except for moving to Oregon or Washington State and the idea of getting a tattoo, I think that every adult (certainly every Baby Boomer) should seriously consider my other suggestions. Getting the legal documents should be a no-brainer.

7. After Death

Some of your legal details will need to be resolved after your death. Documents like deeds, motor vehicle titles, insurance beneficiaries, pensions and tax returns will need to be updated. It is advisable to get as many of these details worked out, even if only as a written guide for loved ones, beforehand.

There is a new after-death phenomenon to contend with. It looks like we will be forever social.

If you have had someone pass away recently, you know that the Internet is now playing a large role in how we remember our deceased friends and family members. Social networks like Facebook are, by their nature, playing an ever-increasing role in death. Our Facebook or LinkedIn page survives our demise (yes, it's a bit weird) and our friends and family can use the deceased's website and their own cyber-memorial to celebrate a life.

I have not given much thought to how I would want to use social networks to deliver personal messages after my death. I may not even choose to do so. And who knows if Facebook will even exist in 19 years. That said, the Internet and social media have clearly opened up a broad new platform for personal storytelling and expression that could, oh no, help us live forever.

With Facebook reporting that well over 200,000 of its members die every year, it is not surprising that there are already social websites specifically designed for us to manage our legacy before we die. The Facebook app If I Die lets you create a final message that gets posted after death, and Evertalk is a website where loved ones can create memorial pages. Given the size of the Baby Boom, there will be more.

I've also considered authoring my own obituary. I'd love mine to be a bit entertaining as well as informative. I use Legacy.com to find ideas. Legacy.com reportedly hosts obituaries and memorials for over 70% of all U.S. deaths. It is among the top 100 most visited sites in the world.

Picking My End-Date

With the easy decisions made, it's time to focus on the most difficult decision: my end-date.

I began this book by asking myself a rather big question: Could I apply rational decision making to create a life-plan that includes my committing suicide? Could I then pick a date for my demise? Could I actually execute this decision? Could I manage the inevitable thoughts and feelings of family and friends when I told them of my plan?

Discovering that I am not the only Baby Boomer who has thought about managing their end-date was one of my most significant research findings. My conversations about this subject with friends and acquaintances revealed that a surprisingly large number of people have given thought to picking an end-date, and a few have actually begun to create end-of-life plans of their own. This is one of those hidden subjects that when brought out in the open can surprise us by being in more people's thoughts than we could ever imagine. The possibility of dying broke and despondent tends to focus the mind. Clearly, the Baby Boomer cohort shares more interests than just a love of classic rock.

I have not been able to find quantitative research to support my hypothesis that an increasing number of older people are contemplating the suicide option. However, we do know that suicide rates are growing within older age groups. In addition to depression and other mental health problems, this increase could be due financial fears and to greater awareness and for some groups, greater acceptance of the idea of physician-assisted suicide, which could be desensitizing us to the idea of suicide itself. Additionally, reduced fear of suicide as a sin, easier access to information on how to commit suicide and the fact that many people do not want to become infirm, die in pain and become a burden to their family could be factors.

One must conclude based on America's very low household net worth statistics, the growing retirement savings deficit and the financial limitations of Social Security, that the majority of my Baby Boomer cohort will be heading for some very lean years just at the time their medical needs and costs increase. With more than 10,000 Baby Boomers reaching 65 each day, it will be interesting to watch the progression of the entitlements debate as it will become the platform for the discussion of aging in America. Unfortunately, our current political stalemate on a range of retirement issues cannot possibly instill any sense of security.

Ultimately, for me, deciding that suicide is a valid and appealing option is the result of very personal beliefs:

I believe that I am solely in control of my life.

I have no sense of personal shame or fear thinking through the suicide option.

I do not fear death and do not yearn for immortality. I don't have what I consider a Magical Mystery Tour perspective on death and an after-life. I don't see myself having a soul that will float up from my body into some cotton candy world where I'll meet all my dead relatives, Plato and Jimi Hendrix. There won't be a test I'll have to pass or a pearly gate to walk through; no gray haired guy in a white suit or even the smiling Buddha to greet me.

Thinking of my saffron-robed friends and the idea of reincarnation, I can't imagine that I might come back as an alpine mountain goat or a monk or, if I've been really good, a New York Yankee. I'm not even sure which one of these reincarnated futures sounds better. I just think I'll stop breathing and that'll be it. Poof. Some might find this a sad perspective but in my worldview, the only thing sad about death is its effect on friends and loved ones and someone dying way too early.

OK, the idea of a life in purgatory is possibly hard for many of us to shake. When I think about why religion designed the concept of eternal Hell, I have to assume that the clergy created it to keep us all in church or simply in line. I'd like to think that the basic premise is societal in nature; If you are a sinner (and suicide is a big sin) or wicked or do really bad deeds that muck up society, then you will live forever in great pain. However, even using this logic, I can't buy it. Just do the math. According to Catholicism, if I do not follow their tenants, I am doomed to eternal damnation. Since Catholics represent approximately 17% of the world's population (according to the Vatican), can we really imagine that 83% of billions of worldwide souls will be forever doomed to live in purgatory? Billions? Even the Dalai Lama? Could this possibly be what God had in mind for all non-Catholics? Conversely, if you are not Muslim are you doomed to live in Jahannam, their Hell? So who is right here? Am I starting to sound a bit, in thoughts but alas not words, like Christopher Hitchens?

Instead of following the teachings of organized religion, my personal philosophy has been to honor the Golden Rule. I have always tried to treat others as I would want them to treat me. Despite my thoughts on Heaven and Hell, if these two afterworlds actually do exist, I'll go with the belief that the Golden Rule will be my ticket to Heaven. Call this my fall back position. See, I do have a moral center; it's just my morality.

Finally, I believe that suicide can be rationally justified.

Remember that I started thinking about the suicide option while reviewing my financial future, particularly the question of how long I could live my personal definition of a happy life. I wondered if the quality of my life could be improved by taking away the vagaries of fate and, importantly, the associated anxieties. Even though I have made a good living, planned for retirement and positioned myself for a few more earning years, there is a point where the money will eventually run out, thus instituting a life where I would wind up living on the kindness of family and Social Security payments. I'm sure many Baby Boomers share this dread of running out of their life savings to depend solely on close to poverty-level Social Security payments and family care.

How long will we live? How much will we need given the costs of dedicated medical communities and high-tech pharmaceuticals? And how long will the unlimited Medicare funds designed to prolong life really last? I find these uncertainties unnerving.

As good storytellers know, emotions trump logic. So, despite my logical arguments thus far, I'm sure you still have one big question:

"Peter, how could you ever seriously consider suicide as an option?"

In the simplest terms: I would like to live worry free for as long as possible. My quality of life is what matters most, not my longevity. Is this selfish? Too "Me generation?" Could be. But, I've been a pampered, self-centered Baby Boomer all of my life and, yes, a hedonist. I would like to maximize living comfortably - and limit pain - in my remaining years. I believe that this is a fair, personal, moral and, simply put, OK decision. Next question.

How long do I want to live? I have chosen my 80th year as my end date. Based on watching people age and my own family's health history, I am fairly sure that 80 is when my body will begin to seriously break down and mobility will diminish at an increasing, even alarming, rate. Eighty is roughly five years before my financial planner projects that I could run out of money. And, well, 80 years on earth seems like a good life. Eighty was also a good end-date for Maude of the 1980's movie Harold and Maude fame. And, perhaps ironically, 80 is the age that the Social Security Administration's Actuarial Life Table says I will bite the dust. Reaching 80 is 19 years away and represents another 25% of my time on earth. I plan to do a lot in my remaining 19 years.

The benefit of making a firm commitment to 80 is that I can be guaranteed a comfortable lifestyle even while spending down my retirement funds. Picking this age ends any anxiety about my future. And it leaves a respectable nest egg for my wife and kids.

My Plan

How and where?

After examining all of the suicide techniques and comparing their success and failure rates, ease (try buying a hand gun in a liberal state), violence, pain and consideration of others, I have determined that three methods merit serious review for my intentions. These methods are based on today's technologies and available methods. It is possible that I could have other options in the future.

The first method I've considered is jumping from the Golden Gate Bridge. This appeals to me for four reasons. I lived in San Francisco and love the bridge and its situation; it is not too far from Portland; it is an efficient method with little room for failure and finally, it is not too messy. However, this route does require some effort and at 80 years of age I might not want or be able to hike out on the bridge to make the big leap over the railing. And, who knows, San Francisco might eventually erect the long planned suicide barrier. Still, this bridge remains an attractive option so who knows.

The second method I've considered is the use of a firearm since it works so well and purchasing a gun is relatively easy and legal for Oregonians. I would use either a shotgun or high caliber handgun with an expanding or hollow-point bullet to increase the likelihood of a fatal shot. However, the use of a gun seems exceedingly violent and inconsiderate of family members and first responders. Plus, although I have lived with western state gun cultures for years, I am a liberal New Yorker at heart. No, using a gun is simply too violent and out of character for me.

That leaves my third and probable method: the helium hood. Available literature says a helium hood is easy to purchase, set up and use as well as being painless and effective. And I am not too worried about today's shortage of helium; I figure the industry will right itself sometime in the next 19 years. I think that this is the way to go, literally.

Now that I've chosen a method, where should I perform my suicide? For me, the question of where comes back to being considerate of others. There is a saying that a single suicide kills more than one person. I respect the fact that no matter how much pre-planning I do, my death will involve other people. Suicide is never a truly solitary act.

The fact is that regardless of methodology (unless I am washed away by San Francisco harbor currents), I will leave a body behind for someone to deal with. I have concluded that first-responders, the police and morticians have chosen to deal with death and are paid to do so. As such, I am more inclined to rely on their experienced services and spare my family from the grim realities.

Today, I can envision heading to a first-floor motel room where I can be alone to set up my helium equipment, spread out some plastic and leave this world peacefully. I'd work hard to plan a way to mitigate issues, especially psychological and emotional issues for those that will be the first to find me. I will also leave a note for hotel staff, as they will play a role regardless of how well I plan my actions. Derek Humphrey, in his book Final Exit, tells of people who have even left large tips. Just in case there is a heaven, I am hopeful that having been a big tipper all my life will deliver some extra points.

My Family

Finally, I am thinking through the best ways to manage my family's feelings. I will have a plan. And yet, no matter how much planning I do, there will be some pain. There is always grief associated with the death of a loved one even if they are terminally ill. My goal is to reduce both the pain and any surprise as much as possible.

I have started to introduce my family to the idea of my taking my life by discussing my thoughts and writing this book. They have 19 years to ask questions, challenge my suppositions, try to change my mind and possibly begin to understand and support my decision. And because it is so far off, I don't intend to belabor the point in daily conversation.

Thus far, my kids have asked some questions that I can't answer. For example, if they have children, will I be able to disregard or dismiss my role as a grandfather, with its privileges and responsibilities? Not being a grandfather today makes this consideration easier to put aside. I just can't deal with this issue right now and hope that it won't be a major determining factor in the future. This is tough stuff, but if I can deal with my wife and kid's feelings, I assume I will be able to do the same with grandchildren.

Generally, my family's current reaction is mixed. They seem to vacillate between outright denial to humor to resignation, all tempered by their knowing that they won't have to deal with the issue any time soon. I have been asked if I plan to let them know the exact date or if I will just quietly head out to my motel one day. I think I'll keep the actual date to myself. I'll just pick one of the 365 days in my 80th year to do the deed. That said, once I hit 80, might they always wonder if my every solo car trip will be one-way? This assumes, of course, that I will still be driving.

Before I go I will write letters expressing my final thoughts and love to family and friends. The most obvious letter will be in the form of a suicide note that I will leave alongside my body. I will make two copies: one for the police and one for the family. It will express the reasons for my suicide and it will state that what I have done is solely my decision and that no one influenced me in any way. I will express that I am going in peace.

So, how do I end the chapter called "The End?"

Whether you agree with my decisions or not, I hope that you at least respect the thought and care I've applied to the subject. I've dug deep into my feelings, defined what is most important to me, researched suicide extensively and talked to like-minded Baby Boomers. Knowing that I am not alone in considering how to end my life is comforting.

I will go at 80. Almost 20 years out.

I will choose a smart, effective and considerate method.

I will have all of my legal affairs in order.

I will have prepared my family as best as I can by having heart-felt discussions of my views. Yes, they have read this book. While this is a path that they can't truly   envision or embrace right now, I think that they understand my desires, perspective and approach. Hopefully, they will be at peace with how I choose to end my personal journey.

I plan to go with a smile. But, can't have that "Last Meal". Well, not too close to my date. It would be a true giveaway.

But Wait, There's More

God and Suicide

As you know by now, I am not religious. However, I have great respect for other people's faith and recognize how important faith is to how people choose to live their lives.

The relationship between religion and suicide is a very complex and personal subject. What follows is, at best (I stress, at best), a top line overview to help put general religious views on suicide into some perspective.

There are centuries of teachings, philosophy and scripture dictating our personal and societal relationship with death and suicide. Such organized religions have direct effects on our moral codes including our general intolerance of suicide because religious teachings forbid it. Hence, to learn countries with larger religious populations have lower suicide rates than those with more secular populations should come as no surprise. Indeed, suicide is viewed as sinful and very bad karma. However, these views have been gradually changing.

In 1980, the New York-based organization Concern for Dying (now known as Choice in Dying), convened a group of psychiatrists, philosophers and theologians who prepared a statement on suicide for the terminally ill:

"Historically, suicide has been judged as sinful by organized religion…We do not dispute the contention that the majority of suicides represent a rejection of the 'gift of life' and, as such, are evidence of severe emotional distress. We believe, however, that a person with a progressive terminal disease faces a unique situation—one which calls for a new look at traditional assumptions about the motivation for choosing suicide.

In our view, this choice might be found to be reasoned, appropriate, altruistic, sacrificial, and loving. We can imagine that an individual faced with debilitating, irreversible illness, who would have to endure intractable pain, mutilating surgery, or demeaning treatments—with added concern for the burden being placed on family and friends—might conclude that suicide was a reasonable, even generous, resolution to a process already moving inexorably toward death."

Despite, changing attitudes about suicide, the act remains a sin in the teachings of all of our major religions.

Buddhism

The Buddhist view of suicide is complex, triggering much scholarly discussion.

On the one hand, Buddhism teaches to avoid the destruction of any life, including one's own. In this light, suicide must logically be seen as an unacceptable action. In Buddhism, the way life ends has a profound impact on the way the new life begins.

On the other hand, the Buddha himself showed tolerance of suicide by Monks in at least two cases where the monks had reached a state of Enlightenment. More recently, the Japanese Buddhist tradition includes many stories of suicides by monks. Some Buddhist Monks have used suicide as a political weapon during the Vietnam War and, more recently, in Myanmar and China.

Christianity

Christians—including Roman Catholics, Protestants, Evangelicals and Baptists—view suicide as a sin. An additional religious impediment to the acceptance of suicide is the common Christian teaching that we are born with a soul and that at end of life we will be judged by God and sent to either Heaven or Hell.

The 4th century Christian philosopher St. Augustine is credited with the first scholarly view that suicide is a sin. He cites the commandment "Thou shalt not kill" as a prohibition to both homicide and suicide. In the 12th century, the theologian Thomas Aquinas wrote that in addition to scriptural prohibitions against suicide, it is unnatural to take our own lives since we are God's creation. In his view, life is a gift from God and therefore to end it is not our right. Aquinas reasoned, "To bring death upon oneself in order to escape the other afflictions of this life is to adopt a greater evil in order to avoid a lesser…Suicide is the most fatal of sins because it cannot be repented of." (Summa Theologica 2-2, q. 64,5)

Hinduism

Like Buddhism, Hinduism has multiple perspectives on suicide but generally views the act as a violation of the code of ahimsa (or non-violence) even if the violence is self-inflicted. In Hinduism, killing interrupts a soul's journey to liberation and brings bad karma. At reincarnation in another physical body, the soul will suffer because the bad karma lives on.

Islam

Islam has similar prohibitions against suicide because the act is an affront to God who has given us life. In the sacred Hadith (the sayings of Muhammad), God is quoted as saying of the one who commits suicide, "My servant has precipitated my will with regard to himself! Therefore, I am forbidding him entry into heaven." If a person is deemed mentally ill at the time of suicide he may be exempted due to his illness and inability to make a rational judgment.

More specifically, according to Abu Huraira (the narrator of Hadith), the Prophet said, "He who commits suicide by throttling shall keep on throttling himself in the Hell-Fire (forever) and he who commits suicide by stabbing himself shall keep on stabbing himself in the Hell-Fire. Whoever purposely throws himself from a mountain and kills himself, will be in the (Hell) Fire falling down into it and abiding therein perpetually forever; and whoever drinks poison and kills himself with it, he will be carrying his poison in his hand and drinking it in the (Hell) Fire wherein he will abide eternally forever; and whoever kills himself with an iron weapon, will be carrying that weapon in his hand and stabbing his abdomen with it in the (Hell) Fire wherein he will abide eternally forever."

Judaism

Jewish law forbids suicide as a matter of accepted practice. Interestingly, however, there are no direct prohibitions of suicide in the Old Testament. Jews do not agree on the nature of an afterlife, and the soul is believed to return to God after death.

Historically, Jews who have committed suicide were buried in a separate part of a Jewish cemetery and were not permitted to receive certain mourning rights. However, in recent times, a more liberal reform view has deemed that people who commit suicide must be mentally ill and/or seriously depressed and therefore not of sound mind. Therefore, some of the older restrictions pertaining to burial have been lifted for non-Orthodox believers.

The Media And Suicide

In a world where traditional and internet-based media plays a large role in shaping our daily views on life and death, I believe that it is important to get some perceptive on how the media presents suicide.

Suicide is a universal topic of interest across the globe. You'll recall that over 7.5 million North Americans search on "suicide" each month. Suicide grips the public's attention and therefore the attention of the media and entertainment industry. In fact, I saw yet another television report on the relationship between cat litter and suicide just this morning. Given all the turmoil in the Middle East, reports on suicide bombers seem to be a weekly occurrence and are a reminder about how we value life.

The media's reporting on suicides has been criticized for a report's potential to incite more suicides by glamourizing the act. Some believe that press coverage, especially when seen by adolescents, creates a copycat effect called the Werther Effect. The Werther Effect suggests that suicides can be inspired by media coverage, reading about successful suicides or having a close friend or relative perform the act. To this point, I imagine the scores of kids that thought about suicide after Nirvana's Kurt Cobain killed himself. The Internet confirms that I am not alone in thinking this; there are over 1.5 million Google results for the phrase "Kurt Cobain Werther Effect."

Sensationalized media treatments of suicide and the rising rate of suicide among American youth resulted in the publication of the 1989 CDC and American Association of Suicidology's guidelines for media coverage of suicide.

The report's guidelines list the following reporting styles that might increase the risk of "copycat" suicides:

- "Presenting oversimplified explanations of suicide, when in fact many factors usually contribute to it. One example concerns the suicide of the widow of a man who was killed in the collapse of the World Trade Center on September 11, 2001. Most newspapers that covered the story described her death as due solely to the act of terrorism, even though she had a history of depressive illness.
- "Excessive, ongoing, or repetitive coverage of the suicide.
- "Sensationalizing the suicide by inclusion of morbid details or dramatic photographs. Some news

accounts of the suicide of an Enron executive in January 2002 are examples of this problem.

- "Giving 'how-to' descriptions of the method of suicide.
- "Referring to suicide as an effective coping strategy or as a way to achieve certain goals.
- "Glorifying the act of suicide or the person who commits suicide.
- "Focusing on the person's positive traits without mentioning his or her problems."

There are over 100 studies examining the relationship between news coverage and suicide rates. In general, suicide rates have been shown to increase after suicides are reported. This is a particularly interesting dilemma for the press and it will be worthwhile to see how this plays out if the incidence of Baby Boomer suicides increases.

A Reading, Viewing and Listening List

In addition to daily media coverage, there have been dozens of books, magazine articles, documentaries, theatrical movies, television and radio shows on death, dying suicide and longevity.

Here is a brief list that I found to be most informative.

Books and Magazines

Amazon lists well over 3,000 books related to the search term suicide. The reader review website Goodreads.com lists over 2,000. After some very careful pruning, six that have helped me the most to understand the subject and how people deal with death itself include:

- Albert Camus' *The Myth of Sisyphus* (1955). The quintessential philosophical examination of man's search for meaning, and an understanding of absurdity and suicide. Camus famously wrote, "There is but one truly serious philosophical problem and that is suicide."

- Carla Fine's *No Time To Say Goodbye: Surviving The Suicide Of A Loved One* (1999). Fine's very personal book recounts her experience with the death of her young physician husband and her pain in not being able to speak openly about her feelings.

- Derek Humphrey's *Final Exit: The Practicalities of Self-Deliverance and Assisted Suicide for the Dying* (1991). Final Exit is viewed by some as a "how to" guide, and therefore is highly controversial. It is one of the frankest books on the subject that I have found.

- Kay Redfield-Jamison's best-selling *Night Falls Fast: Understanding Suicide* (2000). Redfield-Jamison is a prolific John's Hopkins professor of psychiatry who previously wrote *An Unquiet Mind*, a personal memoir about a manic depressive which provides a detailed examination of historical and scientific facts and her educated views on suicide and society's role in it.

- Shelly Kagan's *Death* (The Open Yale Courses Series, 2012). Kagan is a Clark Professor of Philosophy at Yale University. He supports his book with a series of lectures on death and suicide. The book is an exceptional philosophical examination of death, afterlife, mortality and suicide. Kagan's lectures can be seen on the Yale University website and on YouTube. In particular, Suicide, Part I & II: The Rationality of Suicide is an enlightening two-part lecture on the topic of rational suicide.

- Elizabeth Kubler-Ross' *On Death and Dying* (1997). *On Death and Dying* is one of the most famous psychological studies of the late 20th century. The book introduces the idea of the five stages of dealing with death: denial and isolation, anger, bargaining, depression and acceptance.

Beyond the books, I highly recommend four magazine articles that can be read online:

- Sabrina Rubin Erdely's article "One Town's War on Gay Teens," *Rolling Stone* (2012). This is a report on the high numbers of teen suicides exacerbated by the evangelical community's intolerance of an alternative lifestyle. The article provides a liberal view of the relationship between religious views and their potential to cause pain leading to suicide in a vulnerable age group.

- Tad Friend's article "Jumpers – The Fatal Grandeur of the Golden Gate Bridge," *The New Yorker* (2003). The article is a detailed overview of how the Golden Gate Bridge has become one of the most popular suicide destinations.

- Julian J.Z. Prokopetz, B.A., and Lisa Soleymani Lehmann, M.D., Ph.D's article "Redefining Physicians' Role in Assisted Dying," *New England Journal of Medicine* (July 2012). This article is an excellent scholarly overview of the current state of research and opinion on physician-assisted suicide.

- David Samuel's article "Let's Die Together: Why is anonymous group suicide so popular in Japan?," *The Atlantic* (2007). Samuel writes about Internet-led suicide pacts among Japanese youth in 2006 and 2007. According to the Japanese police, over 90 teens and young adults committed suicide after meeting via the web.

Movies and TV

Suicide has been the subject of or played a major role in many movies and television shows. Some of the more famous movies include: *The Virgin Suicides*, *Girl Interrupted*, *The Shawshank Redemption*, *One Flew Over The Cuckoo's Nest* and *Boogie Nights*.

Seven movies and one television show demonstrate the diversity of how the entertainment industry has covered the subject of suicide.

The Ballad of Narayama (1983): In a small Japanese village, everyone who reaches the age of 70 must leave the village and go to a mountaintop to die.

The Bridge (2006): Eric Steel's movie is the most famous and most viewed documentary about suicide. The filmmaker set up his cameras to film one year in the life of the bridge, real time suicides and the personal stories of some who jumped, including a survivor.

Full Metal Jacket (1987): Stanley Kubrick's highly dramatic view of the dehumanizing effects of the Vietnam War on young soldiers. The move includes one of the most graphic movie suicides by the depressed, and seemingly deranged, Marine private Gomer Pyle.

Harold and Maude (1971): Hal Ashby directed this dark comedy and cult-favorite about the joys of life, our inevitable death and the relationship between Harold, a young man obsessed with death and his friend Maude who commits suicide at the end of the movie. Maude believes that 80 is the right age for her to die.

The Self Made Man (2005): Susan Stern's movie tells the story of her 77-year old father Bob and his desire to commit suicide due to a terminal illness. Bob Stern was a successful businessman; husband and father who decided that suicide represented a logical option to waiting for a natural death. It is a poignant and revealing look at how families deal with the rational approach.

How to Die in Oregon (2011): The movie tells the stories of those most intimately involved with the practice of physician-assisted suicide—terminally ill Oregonians, their families, doctors and friends.

"Mad Men – Commission and Fees" (2012): The 2012 season of AMC's Mad Men concluded with a graphic suicide (by hanging) of the depressed advertising executive Lane Pryce.

You Don't Know Jack: The Life and Deaths of Jack Kevorkian (2010): The movie stars Al Pacino in a brilliant performance as the infamous Dr. Death.

Radio

The Philosopher's Zone from Australia's ABC Radio International. A two-part interview on philosophy and suicide with Michael J. Cholbi, Associate Professor from the Department of Philosophy at California State Polytechnic University.

The Suicide Paradox: a New Freakonomics Radio Podcast (2011). A fascinating, information-rich podcast that includes interviews with some of America's leading suicide experts.

Some Famous Suicides

We are fascinated by famous suicides. These suicides by people that we know only by reputation appear to satisfy some innate prurient interest and may act as a kind of mirror for our own demons.

Individual Suicides

Diane Arbus (1971), American photographer who overdosed on pills and slashed wrists.

Cleopatra (30 BC), the Queen of Egypt, induced a snake to bite her.

Kurt Cobain (1994), an American rock singer (Nirvana), killed himself with a shotgun blast to the head.

Don Cornelius (2012), an American television show host and producer best known as the creator and host of the nationally syndicated dance/music franchise Soul Train, shot himself.

George Eastman (1932), an American inventor (Kodak) and philanthropist, died via a self-inflicted gunshot to the heart.

Arshile Gorky (1948), an Armenian-born American painter, died from hanging.

Vincent van Gough (1890), the famous Dutch painter, shot himself.

Spalding Gray (2004), an American actor, playwright, screenwriter, performance artist and monologist, jumped off of the Staten Island Ferry.

Ernest Hemingway (1961), an American writer and journalist, gunshot wound to the head.

Margaux Hemmingway (1996), an American fashion model and actress, overdosed on phenobarbital.

Frida Kahlo (1954), a Mexican painter, from killed herself via a drug overdose. She wrote, "I hope the exit is joyful — and I hope never to return — Frida."

Jerzy Kosinski (1991), a Polish-born American writer, suffocated himself with a plastic bag.

Yukio Mishima (1975), a Japanese author, poet, playwright, actor and film director, famously committed suicide by seppuku, a ritual Japanese suicide by sword.

Sylvia Plath (1963), an American poet, novelist and children's author, committed suicide by gassing herself in her kitchen.

Mark Rothko (1970), an American abstract expressionist painter, slit his arms and bled to death.

Junior Seau (2012), an All-Pro American football player, died via a self-inflicted gunshot to the chest.

Tony Scott (2012), an American film director, jumped from a Los Angles bridge.

Alan Turning (1954), an English mathematician, logician, cryptanalyst and computer scientist, ate an apple laced with cyanide.

Dan White (1985), a San Francisco politician who assassinated Mayor George Moscone and Harvey Milk, killed himself via carbon monoxide poisoning.

Virginia Woolf (1941), an English author, essayist, publisher and writer of short stories, committed suicide by drowning.

Group Suicides

History has seen many mass suicides. Three stand out to me for their continued fascination years later.

Masada – In 73 AD, 960 members of the Sicarii group living in Masada killed themselves despite Jewish laws against suicide. Their actions were motivated by Roman threats. According to historical accounts, each man killed his family and then turned on each other.

The Masada event has taken on symbolic meaning for the persecuted because it was the last stand of Jewish freedom fighters against the powerful Roman army.

Jonestown – On November 18, 1978, 912 followers of Reverend James Warren Jones followed his instructions to drink a deadly purple punch laced with cyanide, sedatives and tranquilizers. After the suicides, Jones shot himself in the head.

Earlier, concerns among the cult's American family members led to the televised visit by California Congressman Leo Ryan. Ryan's life was threatened during the visit, so he fled to the airport where he and four members of his team were ambushed and killed. After the murder, Jones convinced his followers that their idyllic life was over and commanded them to die together.

Kamikaze – Kamikazes, or Divine Wind in Japanese, were Japanese navy airmen that used their aircraft as self-propelled missiles to target allied warships near the end of World War II.

These suicidal attacks began in October 1944 after the Japanese began to experience large combat loses. They had long lost aerial dominance due to outdated aircraft and the loss of experienced pilots.

The best estimates state that around 50 Allied warships ranging from small PT boats to aircraft carriers were sunk at the hands of kamikaze pilots. Approximately 300 additional warships were damaged.

The term kamikaze is now used to describe other intentional combat and terrorist suicide attacks.

The Compassionate: Suicide Organizations

If you are interested in gaining a deeper understanding about the right-to-die and assisted-suicide movements, I recommend that you spend some time reviewing the information on the following websites:

Oregon Death with Dignity Act - From the Oregon Health Authority

"On October 27, 1997 Oregon enacted the Death with Dignity Act (the Act) which allows terminally-ill Oregonians to end their lives through the voluntary self-administration of lethal medications, expressly prescribed by a physician for that purpose. The Act requires the Oregon Public Health Division to collect information about the patients and physicians who participate in the Act and publish an annual statistical report. These data are important to parties on both sides of the issue. Our position is a neutral one, and we offer no opinions about these questions. We routinely receive inquiries about the Act."

Death With Dignity:

"The greatest human freedom is to live, and die, according to one's own desires and beliefs. From advance directives to physician-assisted dying, death with dignity is a movement to provide options for the dying to control their own end-of-life care.

"Death with Dignity National Center is the leader in this movement, successfully establishing, advancing and defending the landmark Oregon and Washington Death with Dignity Acts."

The Final Exit Network:

"We hold that mentally competent adults have a basic human right to end their lives under the following conditions:

"They suffer from a fatal or irreversible illness or intractable pain,

"They judge that their quality of life is unacceptable to them,

"They judge that their future is hopeless.

"This right by its nature implies that the ending of one's life is one's choice, including the timing and persons present, and should be free of any restrictions by the law, clergy, medical profession, etc. We do not encourage anyone to end their life, are opposed to anyone's encouraging another to end his life, do not provide the means to do so, and do not assist in a person's death. We do, however, support any member who requests it when they meet our official, written criteria."

For updated details on legal issues pertaining to suicide and assisted-suicides on a state-by-state basis, visit the CQ StateTrack legislative website.

World Federation of Right To Die Societies

"The World Federation, founded in 1980, consists of 46 right to die organizations from 25 countries. The Federation provides an international link for organizations working to secure or protect the rights of individuals to self-determination at the end of their lives."

The Author

Baby Boomer Peter Levitan grew up in Manhattan in the 50s and 60s, went to Woodstock and has lived in Massachusetts, California, Minnesota, New Jersey, Oregon and London, England. He stumped the panel on television's *To Tell The Truth* by claiming to be a National Science Award winner who experimented with LSD on spiders. And he represented his Baby Boom generation on the short-lived TV show *The Generation Gap*.

Levitan's 40 years in business include owning a San Francisco photography studio, global management positions at Saatchi & Saatchi Advertising Worldwide (the world's largest agency), founding two Internet companies and owning an Oregon-based advertising and design agency with clients that included Nike, Harrah's, Dr. Martins and the United Nations. In 1999, he was named the Newspaper Association of America's "New Media Pioneer."

Boomercide: From Woodstock to Suicide is just the beginning of what will be an evolving series of books and blog entries about the 76 million Baby Boomers: our history, dreams, factoids and sound advice on how to make our future groovier.

Visit Peter online and share your opinions on his views, rants and this book at his website, www.peterlevitan.com.

As a bonus, just like with Ginsu Knife commercials, "there's more!" Peter's website gives you exclusive access to his informative how-to essay, "How I wrote and published my first book in three months." He thinks that in this day of digital books, we all have the tools to tell our own story.